WEEKLY WR READER®
EARLY LEARNING LIBRARY

➕ SAFETY FIRST

Staying Safe
In the Car

by Joanne Mattern

Reading consultant: Susan Nations, M.Ed.,
author/literacy coach/consultant in literacy development

Please visit our web site at: www.garethstevens.com
For a free color catalog describing Weekly Reader® Early Learning Library's list
of high-quality books, call 1-877-445-5824 (USA) or 1-800-387-3178 (Canada).
Weekly Reader® Early Learning Library's fax: (414) 336-0164.

Library of Congress Cataloging-in-Publication Data

Mattern, Joanne, 1963-
     Staying safe in the car / by Joanne Mattern.
         p. cm. — (Safety first)
     Includes bibliographical references and index.
     ISBN-13: 978-0-8368-7793-9 (lib. bdg.)
     ISBN-13: 978-0-8368-7800-4 (softcover)
     1. Transportation—Safety measures—Juvenile literature.   2. Automobiles—Safety Measures—
Juvenile literature.   3. Automobiles—Seat belts—Juvenile literature.   4. Safety Education—
Juvenile literature.   I. Title.
     HE194.M39   2007
     613.6'8—dc22
                                                                        2006030335

This edition first published in 2007 by
Weekly Reader® Early Learning Library
A Member of the WRC Media Family of Companies
330 West Olive Street, Suite 100
Milwaukee, WI 53212 USA

Copyright © 2007 by Weekly Reader® Early Learning Library

Managing editor: Valerie J. Weber
Editor: Barbara Kiely Miller
Art direction: Tammy West
Cover design and page layout: Charlie Dahl
Picture research: Diane Laska-Swanke
Photographer: Jack Long

The publisher thanks Mya, Tyler, and Ramon Salinas; and Mary Ann Zawlocki for their
assistance with this book.

Printed in the United States of America

1 2 3 4 5 6 7 8 9 10 10 09 08 07 06

2607253

Note to Educators and Parents

Reading is such an exciting adventure for young children! They are beginning to integrate their oral language skills with written language. To encourage children along the path to early literacy, books must be colorful, engaging, and interesting; they should invite the young reader to explore both the print and the pictures.

The *Safety First* series is designed to help young readers review basic safety rules, learn new vocabulary, and strengthen their reading comprehension. In simple, easy-to-read language, each book teaches children to stay safe in an everyday situation such as at home, at school, or in the outside world.

Each book is specially designed to support the young reader in the reading process. The familiar topics are appealing to young children and invite them to read — and reread — again and again. The full-color photographs and enhanced text further support the student during the reading process.

In addition to serving as wonderful picture books in schools, libraries, homes, and other places where children learn to love reading, these books are specifically intended to be read within an instructional guided reading group. This small group setting allows beginning readers to work with a fluent adult model as they make meaning from the text. After children develop fluency with the text and content, the book can be read independently. Children and adults alike will find these books supportive, engaging, and fun!

— Susan Nations, M.Ed., author, literacy coach,
and consultant in literacy development

A car can take us to many fun places. Do you know how to ride safely in the car?

Car seats help children stay safe. Big kids can ride in **booster seats**.

booster seat

Children should always ride
in the back seat.

You must always wear a **seat belt**. It will keep you safe in an **accident**.

seat belt

A seat belt should fit across your **shoulder** and chest. Make sure it is tight. Then **buckle** up!

shoulder

buckle

13

Keep your hands and head
inside the car.

Talk softly and play quietly during the ride.

When the car stops, open the door near the sidewalk. Do not step into the street.

sidewalk

19

Let's go for a safe ride
in the car!

Glossary

accident — a sudden event that might hurt somebody

booster seats — special safety seats for children ages five to eight to use in a car

buckle — to connect two straps together with a metal clip, also called a buckle

car seats — special safety seats for children younger than five to use in a car

seat belt — a strap that holds a person tightly in a seat, such as in a car

shoulder — the part of your body between your neck and your upper arm

For More Information

Books

Safety Signs. Scott Peters (Benchmark Education)

Signs on the Road. Signs in My World (series). Mary Hill (Children's Press)

Traffic Safety. Safety Sense (series). Nancy Loewen (Child's World)

Watch Out! On the Road. Watch Out! Books (series). Claire Llewellyn (Barron's Educational)

Web Sites

Car Seat and Seat Belt Kids Page
www.nysgtsc.state.ny.us/Kids/kid-seat.htm
This site has a fun jigsaw puzzle and explains how seat belts and car seats keep you safe.

Help Keep Kids Safe
www.helpkeepkidssafe.org/kt_kids_tips_aut.html
Questions and tips to help keep kids safe while riding in a car

Publisher's note to educators and parents: Our editors have carefully reviewed these Web sites to ensure that they are suitable for children. Many Web sites change frequently, however, and we cannot guarantee that a site's future contents will continue to meet our high standards of quality and educational value. Be advised that children should be closely supervised whenever they access the Internet.

Index

About the Author

Joanne Mattern has written more than 150 books for children. She has written about weird animals, sports, world cities, dinosaurs, and many other subjects. Joanne also works in her local library. She lives in New York State with her husband, three daughters, and assorted pets. She enjoys animals, music, going to baseball games, reading, and visiting schools to talk about her books.